THE FAMILY PRAYERBOOK

Shabbat

SHELDON ZIMMERMAN

Illustrations by

ELEANOR SCHICK

Rossel Books
Dallas, Texas

© Copyright 1991 by Temple Emanu-El of Dallas, Texas

All rights reserved.

*Our gratitude to Seymour Rossel for his thoughtful, spiritual,
and creative editing and guidance;
and to Susan Salom for her caring help.*

*ISBN 0-940646-61-7
Typesetting and Design by R.C.C.*

Distributed by
BEHRMAN HOUSE, INC.
235 Watchung Avenue
West Orange, NJ 07052

*For Judy, Brian, Kira,
David & Micol
and all the children and
families of Temple Emanu-El
S.Z.*

**The publication of this prayerbook is made
possible through the generosity of
Rhea Fay Fruhman,
in memory of Leo Fruhman
and Leonard Fruhman**

CONTENTS

Shabbat Evening
    Service I   7
    Service II   17
Shabbat Morning Service   25
Torah Service   33
Closing Prayers   37
Havdalah   43

SHABBAT EVENING
Service I

Shabbat is a day of sounds: The sounds we make as we clean our rooms to get them ready for Shabbat. The sounds we make as we bring our best dishes to the Shabbat table. The sounds of chanting the *kiddush*. The sounds of singing Shabbat songs together.

Shabbat is a day of many sounds.

Some sounds are splendid — other sounds ache and sting.

Our ears can hurt when we play stereos too loudly.

Our ears can hurt when we are very noisy.

At times we are angry and yell at other people;

At times cars and machines make too much noise.

Sometimes the noise we make is so great, we can hardly hear ourselves at all.

Shabbat is a day of many sounds — but the finest sound of Shabbat is the sound of silence. Try to be silent for a moment now. Think of the quiet beauty of Shabbat. Try to feel the sound of family and friends all around. And remember that feeling as we welcome Shabbat with the sweet sound of Shabbat songs.

בִּם, בָּם, שַׁבָּת שָׁלוֹם.

Bim, bam, Shabbat Shalom.

מַה יָפֶה הַיוֹם, שַׁבָּת שָׁלוֹם.

Ma yafeh ha-yom, Shabbat Shalom.

There are times we want to say something important to our parents, our children, our sisters, our brothers, or our friends. We could yell it out — but somehow that just doesn't seem right. What we have to say is too important for yelling or screaming.

Instead we become very quiet. We whisper. People listen when we speak gently because they know that important things are shared quietly.

Shabbat is like a gentle whisper. It says important things to each of us — but it says them quietly. It says: "Listen to what you are thinking." "Listen to what you are saying inside of you." "Listen to your heart." And "Listen to your mind, not just to what's outside." It says: "Listen to your parents." "Listen to your children." "What are they really saying?" It says: "Listen to God." "What is God saying to us?" Tonight let's try to listen to Shabbat, to ourselves, to our parents, children, and friends; and let us try to listen to God.

ALL RISE

בָּרְכוּ אֶת יְיָ הַמְבֹרָךְ.

Let us praise God.

בָּרוּךְ יְיָ הַמְבֹרָךְ לְעוֹלָם וָעֶד.

We praise God now and forever.

FOR GOD'S CREATION

Baruch atah Adonai — We Praise You, *Adonai*,
   For the amazing universe of which we are a part.
For the glory of daybreak; for the quietude of nightfall;
   For the order of nature, season following season.

בָּרוּךְ אַתָּה, יְיָ, הַמַּעֲרִיב עֲרָבִים.

We praise You, O God, for the order of night and day,
   for the twilight and for the wonder of our lives.

FOR THE GIFT OF TORAH

With a great love You love us, O God,
   Your Torah is a light for our path, a guide for our lives.
May our eyes grow bright in the study of Your Torah.
   May our hearts and actions be faithful to Your *mitzvot*.
May we learn to love You as You love us.
   We thank You O God, for giving us the Torah, Your most precious gift.
We thank You, O God, for Your Torah, Your great gift of love.

THE SHEMA

שְׁמַע יִשְׂרָאֵל: יְיָ אֱלֹהֵינוּ, יְיָ אֶחָד.

Hear, O Israel: The Lord is our God, the Lord is One.

בָּרוּךְ שֵׁם כְּבוֹד מַלְכוּתוֹ לְעוֹלָם וָעֶד.

Praised be God whose Rule is forever.

וְאָהַבְתָּ אֵת יְיָ אֱלֹהֶיךָ בְּכָל־לְבָבְךָ וּבְכָל־נַפְשְׁךָ וּבְכָל־מְאֹדֶךָ. וְהָיוּ הַדְּבָרִים הָאֵלֶּה, אֲשֶׁר אָנֹכִי מְצַוְּךָ הַיּוֹם, עַל־לְבָבֶךָ. וְשִׁנַּנְתָּם לְבָנֶיךָ, וְדִבַּרְתָּ בָּם בְּשִׁבְתְּךָ בְּבֵיתֶךָ, וּבְלֶכְתְּךָ בַדֶּרֶךְ וּבְשָׁכְבְּךָ וּבְקוּמֶךָ.

וּקְשַׁרְתָּם לְאוֹת עַל־יָדֶךָ. וְהָיוּ לְטֹטָפֹת בֵּין עֵינֶיךָ. וּכְתַבְתָּם עַל־מְזֻזוֹת בֵּיתֶךָ. וּבִשְׁעָרֶיךָ.

לְמַעַן תִּזְכְּרוּ וַעֲשִׂיתֶם אֶת־כָּל־מִצְוֹתָי. וִהְיִיתֶם קְדֹשִׁים לֵאלֹהֵיכֶם. אֲנִי יְיָ אֱלֹהֵיכֶם. אֲשֶׁר הוֹצֵאתִי אֶתְכֶם מֵאֶרֶץ מִצְרַיִם לִהְיוֹת לָכֶם לֵאלֹהִים. אֲנִי יְיָ אֱלֹהֵיכֶם.

You shall love *Adonai* your God
    With all your strength and mind.
These words which I command you today –
    Keep them close to your heart.
Teach them to your children,
    Say them over and again.
In the evening and in the morning,
    Wherever you may be,
When you speak, when you are silent,
    Keep them close, very close.
Copy these words;
    Set them before you.

On the doorposts of your homes,
> **And on your gates.**

So that you will remember your God
> **And do all of God's commandments,**

Today and every day of your life.

FOR THE PROMISE OF REDEMPTION

בָּרוּךְ אַתָּה, יְיָ, גָּאַל יִשְׂרָאֵל.

We remember a time long before we were born,
> **Our people left the Holy Land to settle in the land of Egypt.**

Then Pharaoh and his people enslaved us—
> **They forced us to work as slaves and robbed us of our freedom.**

With an outstretched arm and a mighty hand, God brought us out of Egypt.
> **God taught us to hate slavery and love freedom.**

To act in the Image of God, we must do what God has done.
> **We must set the captive free; we must rescue the slave from slavery.**

Baruch atah, Adonai, Ga-al Yisrael.
> **We praise You, *Adonai* — Redeemer of Israel.**

THE COMMAND TO OBSERVE AND REMEMBER

The Jewish people shall observe Shabbat always. It is unique, a day we keep as a *brit olam* — an eternal covenant.
> **Shabbat is a sign — reminding us that God worked six days to create the world.**

Shabbat is a sign — reminding us that God rested on the seventh day, making Creation complete.
> **We, too, must work — using our minds and hands, our ideas and our abilities to create as God creates.**

We, too, must rest — stop what we're doing, look at what we've done, and say, as God said, "It is good."

On the seventh day — Shabbat — God stopped and looked around.

God rested; and God blessed the Shabbat day, calling it "the Day of Rest."

וְשָׁמְרוּ בְנֵי־יִשְׂרָאֵל אֶת־הַשַּׁבָּת. לַעֲשׂוֹת אֶת־הַשַּׁבָּת לְדֹרֹתָם בְּרִית עוֹלָם.

בֵּינִי וּבֵין בְּנֵי יִשְׂרָאֵל אוֹת הִיא לְעֹלָם. כִּי שֵׁשֶׁת יָמִים עָשָׂה יְיָ

אֶת־הַשָּׁמַיִם וְאֶת־הָאָרֶץ. וּבַיּוֹם הַשְּׁבִיעִי שָׁבַת וַיִּנָּפַשׁ.

TEFILLAH

We praise You, *Adonai*, our God, God of our Fathers and Mothers, God of all generations. Your ways are loving as you heal the sick and free the captive, as you send help to the falling and comfort all who suffer pain.

We praise You, O God,
   For the holiness of the world,
For the holiness of Shabbat,
   For the holiness of life.
We praise You, O God,
   Source of holiness.
Baruch atah, Adonai, ha-el hakadosh.

MAY WE REJOICE – KEDUSHAT HAYOM

We rest on Shabbat,
   We think on Shabbat.
We spend more time with family and friends,
   We spend more time in prayer.

But Shabbat is much more than a day of thinking and of praying.
   Shabbat is a day of joy, a day of happiness.
We sing, we dance, we laugh, we embrace;
   We celebrate the joys of friendship, love, family.
It is wonderful to be alive,
   It is wonderful to celebrate Shabbat.
Baruch atah, Adonai, mekadesh hashabbat.
   We Praise You, O God, Who makes the Shabbat holy,
Who sanctifies the Shabbat.

WORSHIP, THANKSGIVING, AND PEACE

Thank You, God, for family and friends.
   Thank You, God, for all the wonderful moments and people in my life.
Thank You, God, for the opportunity to worship and pray in this beautiful place.
   Thank You, God, for filling our world with beauty.
Now help us work for *Shalom* — Your blessing and gift of peace.
   We know that even when it feels like *Shalom* is a distant dream,
You promised that peace can be real, if only we strive for it and seek it out.
   Shabbat is a day of peace.
All days can become like Shabbat — if together we work for *Shalom*.
   Shabbat is a promise.

A promise that someday soon there will be *Shalom* — for You, for me, for our people in Israel, for all people everywhere. *Shabbat Shalom* — Shabbat, the day of peace, is the promise for peace for all of us.

[A SHABBAT SONG]

We close our eyes and pray quietly, saying words without sound.

SILENT PRAYER

**May the words of my mouth echo God's words,
May the thoughts in my heart ever be thoughts of God.** *Amen.*

SERMON

(TORAH SERVICE: PAGE 35)

CLOSING PRAYERS: PAGE 39

SHABBAT EVENING
Service II

Welcome Shabbat!

Whenever we want to do something special we spend time getting ready. We change our clothes, straighten our rooms, brush our hair and check ourselves in the mirror.

Shabbat is a special day, a different day. To welcome Shabbat we need to get ready. We dress up nicely. We gather together. But we still are not ready.

We need to get close to each other. Shabbat is a day for coming closer; Shabbat is a day for hugging. Turn to the person next to you. Take your neighbor's hand and say,

"*Shabbat Shalom!* Shabbat Peace!"
    "***Shabbat Shalom!* Shabbat Peace!**"
"I am glad to see you here."
    "**I am glad to see you here.**"
"I am pleased that you are with me."
    "**I am pleased that you are with me.**"
"*Shabbat Shalom!* Shabbat Peace!"
    "***Shabbat Shalom!* Shabbat Peace!**"

[A SHABBAT SONG]

To celebrate beautiful moments, we create light.
    At our birthday parties, we light candles on the birthday cake.
On Hanukkah, we light candles on our *Hanukkiah* — our Hanukkah *Menorah*.
    At every Jewish holiday we light candles.

Shabbat, too, is a holiday — but it is different. Other holidays come only once a year; Shabbat comes once each week. Every week we light Shabbat candles. We say "Welcome Shabbat!"

"Welcome Shabbat!" Welcome to our Temple and to our homes.
    "Welcome Shabbat!" Welcome to our hearts and to our lives.

ALL:

בָּרוּךְ אַתָּה, יְיָ אֱלֹהֵינוּ, מֶלֶךְ הָעוֹלָם, אֲשֶׁר קִדְּשָׁנוּ בְּמִצְוֹתָיו, וְצִוָּנוּ לְהַדְלִיק נֵר שֶׁל שַׁבָּת.

Baruch atah, Adonai — **We praise You,** *Adonai* —
whose *mitzvot* **make us holy** —
for the *mitzvah* **of lighting and blessing
the Shabbat candles.**

See the beautiful lights,
   Shabbat is here again.
Shabbat is a day of brightness,
   Even the taste of Shabbat is sweet.
We lift the kiddush cup filled with wine,
   Symbol of sweetness, the taste of Shabbat.

בָּרוּךְ אַתָּה, יְיָ אֱלֹהֵינוּ, מֶלֶךְ הָעוֹלָם, בּוֹרֵא פְּרִי הַגָּפֶן.

Baruch atah, Adonai — **We praise You,** *Adonai* —
Ruler of the universe, Creator of the fruit of the vine.

The songs, the candles, the wine — we are ready now
   To praise God, to thank *Adonai,*
For life, for health, for Shabbat.

ALL RISE

בָּרְכוּ אֶת יְיָ הַמְבֹרָךְ.
Let us praise God.

בָּרוּךְ יְיָ הַמְבֹרָךְ לְעוֹלָם וָעֶד.
We praise God now and forever.

Shabbat is a day for saying, "Thank you." Often we take people for granted. We forget to say, "Thank you." We really meant to say it . . .

We just forgot. We were busy. We were thinking ahead: About other people, other things. Shabbat says, "Stop. Think about your life. Think about your parents, your children, your friends, your home."

Shabbat says, It is time to say "thank you" for each other —

Thank you! For our lives — Thank you!

For our world — Thank you!

For our Temple — Thank you!

For our children — Thank you!

For our parents — Thank you!

For all of life — Thank you!

Thank you, God!

Thank you, God!

THE SHEMA

שְׁמַע יִשְׂרָאֵל: יְיָ אֱלֹהֵינוּ, יְיָ אֶחָד.

Hear, O Israel: The Lord is our God, the Lord is One.

בָּרוּךְ שֵׁם כְּבוֹד מַלְכוּתוֹ לְעוֹלָם וָעֶד.

Praised be God whose Rule is forever.

וְאָהַבְתָּ אֵת יְיָ אֱלֹהֶיךָ בְּכָל־לְבָבְךָ וּבְכָל־נַפְשְׁךָ וּבְכָל־מְאֹדֶךָ. וְהָיוּ הַדְּבָרִים הָאֵלֶּה, אֲשֶׁר אָנֹכִי מְצַוְּךָ הַיּוֹם, עַל־לְבָבֶךָ. וְשִׁנַּנְתָּם לְבָנֶיךָ, וְדִבַּרְתָּ בָּם בְּשִׁבְתְּךָ בְּבֵיתֶךָ, וּבְלֶכְתְּךָ בַדֶּרֶךְ וּבְשָׁכְבְּךָ וּבְקוּמֶךָ.

וּקְשַׁרְתָּם לְאוֹת עַל־יָדֶךָ, וְהָיוּ לְטֹטָפֹת בֵּין עֵינֶיךָ. וּכְתַבְתָּם עַל־מְזֻזוֹת בֵּיתֶךָ, וּבִשְׁעָרֶיךָ.

לְמַעַן תִּזְכְּרוּ וַעֲשִׂיתֶם אֶת־כָּל־מִצְוֹתָי. וִהְיִיתֶם קְדֹשִׁים לֵאלֹהֵיכֶם. אֲנִי יְיָ אֱלֹהֵיכֶם, אֲשֶׁר הוֹצֵאתִי אֶתְכֶם מֵאֶרֶץ מִצְרַיִם לִהְיוֹת לָכֶם לֵאלֹהִים. אֲנִי יְיָ אֱלֹהֵיכֶם.

You shall love *Adonai* your God
> **With all your strength and mind.**

These words which I command you today —
> **Keep them close to your heart.**

Teach them to your children,
> **Say them over and again.**

In the evening and in the morning,
> **Wherever you may be,**

When you speak, when you are silent,
> **Keep them close, very close.**

Copy these words;
> **Set them before you.**

On the doorposts of your homes,
> **And on your gates.**

So that you will remember your God
> **And do all of God's commandments,**

Today and every day of your life.

[A SHABBAT SONG]

Shabbat is a day of thinking. We think about people we care about. We think about the past week. How did we behave? How did we show the people we love that we love them? How did we do what we wanted to do? Sometimes we are proud of what we did; sometimes not.

Shabbat is a day of thinking.
> **We think about how to behave.**

Shabbat is a day of thinking.
> **Temple is a place for thinking.**

Shabbat helps us to grow and change,
> **To change — and, by changing, to grow.**

[A SHABBAT SONG]

When we are quiet we can think. Sometimes even our spoken prayers become too noisy. We need quiet time. Now—in this space—in the quietness of our hearts—let us think and pray.

SILENT PRAYER

May the words of our mouths and the meditations of our hearts be acceptable in Your sight, O God, Our Rock and Redeemer. Amen.

SERMON

(TORAH SERVICE: PAGE 35)

CLOSING PRAYERS: PAGE 39

Shabbat is a day of closeness.
> **Shabbat is a day of hugging.**

There are times when we really need a hug,
> **We just forget to ask.**

Sometimes parents understand;
> **They hug us tightly.**

Sometimes parents are busy being adults,
> **They walk by us and seem to forget we are there.**

Sometimes our children understand;
> **They hug us tightly.**

Sometimes children are busy with games or friends,
> **They walk by us and seem to forget we are there.**

On Shabbat we are ready. Now we feel very close to each other. Shabbat is a day of closeness. Shabbat is a day of hugging. Give each other a Shabbat hug. *"Shabbat Shalom."*

Holding hands we leave, to continue enjoying God's special day. *"Shabbat Shalom."*

SHABBAT MORNING SERVICE

Daylight brightens our world. The darkness of night retreats, the morning light brings hope and anticipation.

**We thank you God for the night and its rest;
and for this new morning with its light and hope.**

מוֹדֶה אֲנִי לְפָנֶיךָ, מֶלֶךְ חַי וְקַיָּם,
שֶׁהֶחֱזַרְתָּ בִּי נִשְׁמָתִי בְּחֶמְלָה, רַבָּה אֱמוּנָתֶךָ.

But this is more than just another weekday morning. This is *Shabbat* morning—a time to come closer to God, to chant ancient prayers, to come closer to family and friends. *Mah yafeh hayom*—how beautiful this day can be—*Shabbat shalom*.

מַה יָּפֶה הַיּוֹם, שַׁבָּת שָׁלוֹם.

We come together on this day as a special group—a holy community. Many mornings we spend with friends. We study at school together, we play sports together. Today, we are a holy community. We gather to pray, to study, to come closer to God—to become a holy nation. The Jewish people are a holy people. Let us make our way then to holiness. Let us call each other to prayer and to study.

ALL RISE

בָּרְכוּ אֶת יְיָ הַמְבֹרָךְ.
Let us praise God.

בָּרוּךְ יְיָ הַמְבֹרָךְ לְעוֹלָם וָעֶד.
We praise God now and forever.

O God, you are so loving to us.
   You created our world, filled with warmth, sunshine, and beauty.
O God, you are so loving to us.
   You created night and day, all the order which is part of our lives.
O God, you are so loving to us.
   You created the sun, moon, and stars—the light that brightens our lives.

O God, you are so loving to us.

> You created men and women to be like You: loving, caring and creating, making this world a better place.

בָּרוּךְ אַתָּה, יְיָ, יוֹצֵר הַמְּאוֹרוֹת.

We praise You, O God, for the brightness of the skies.

בָּרוּךְ אַתָּה, יְיָ, בּוֹרֵא אֶת הַכֹּל.

> We praise You, O God, for all the wonderful things and for our world which You have created.

O God, you are so loving to us.

> You brought us to Mount Sinai and gave us the Torah.

O God, you are so loving to us.

> You gave us the Torah to teach us how to live, how to become better people.

בָּרוּךְ אַתָּה, יְיָ, הַבּוֹחֵר בְּעַמּוֹ יִשְׂרָאֵל בְּאַהֲבָה.

> We praise You, O God, for loving us so much that You have given us Your Torah.

And now we accept You as our God, and Your Torah as our Torah. We thank you by calling You our God and proclaiming You One.

THE SHEMA

שְׁמַע יִשְׂרָאֵל: יְיָ אֱלֹהֵינוּ, יְיָ אֶחָד.

Hear, O Israel: The Lord is our God, the Lord is One.

בָּרוּךְ שֵׁם כְּבוֹד מַלְכוּתוֹ לְעוֹלָם וָעֶד.

Praised be God whose Rule is forever.

וְאָהַבְתָּ אֵת יְיָ אֱלֹהֶיךָ בְּכָל־לְבָבְךָ וּבְכָל־נַפְשְׁךָ וּבְכָל־מְאֹדֶךָ. וְהָיוּ הַדְּבָרִים הָאֵלֶּה, אֲשֶׁר אָנֹכִי מְצַוְּךָ הַיּוֹם, עַל־לְבָבֶךָ. וְשִׁנַּנְתָּם לְבָנֶיךָ. וְדִבַּרְתָּ בָּם בְּשִׁבְתְּךָ בְּבֵיתֶךָ, וּבְלֶכְתְּךָ בַדֶּרֶךְ וּבְשָׁכְבְּךָ וּבְקוּמֶךָ.

וּקְשַׁרְתָּם לְאוֹת עַל־יָדֶךָ, וְהָיוּ לְטֹטָפֹת בֵּין עֵינֶיךָ.
וּכְתַבְתָּם עַל־מְזֻזוֹת בֵּיתֶךָ, וּבִשְׁעָרֶיךָ.

לְמַעַן תִּזְכְּרוּ וַעֲשִׂיתֶם אֶת־כָּל־מִצְוֹתָי. וִהְיִיתֶם קְדֹשִׁים לֵאלֹהֵיכֶם.
אֲנִי יְיָ אֱלֹהֵיכֶם. אֲשֶׁר הוֹצֵאתִי אֶתְכֶם מֵאֶרֶץ מִצְרַיִם
לִהְיוֹת לָכֶם לֵאלֹהִים.   אֲנִי יְיָ אֱלֹהֵיכֶם.

You shall love *Adonai* your God
    With all your strength and mind.
These words which I command you today —
    Keep them close to your heart.
Teach them to your children,
    Say them over and again.
In the evening and in the morning,
    Wherever you may be,
When you speak, when you are silent,
    Keep them close, very close.
Copy these words;
    Set them before you.
On the doorposts of your homes,
    And on your gates.
So that you will remember your God
    And do all of God's commandments,
Today and every day of your life.

O God, you are so loving to us.
    We remember when we were slaves in Egypt. You set us free.
O God, you are so loving to us.
    **Now when we see people trapped by hurt or suffering, we know
        You will remember them.**
O God, you are so loving to us.
    We know that someday all people will be free.

O God, you are so loving to us.

> Our brothers and sisters in Israel and our people throughout the world — all will be safe and free.

בָּרוּךְ אַתָּה, יְיָ, גָּאַל יִשְׂרָאֵל.

> **We praise You, O God, for delivering us from Egypt and promising to deliver us in the future again.**

TEFILLAH

We praise You, *Adonai*, our God, God of our Fathers and Mothers, God of all generations. Your ways are loving as you heal the sick and free the captive, as you send help to the falling and comfort all who suffer pain.

KEDUSHAH

You are a holy God who calls us to be holy — a God who is different from the other gods that ancient people worshipped. We call you, *HaKadosh*, the Holy One, as did the prophet Isaiah thousands of years ago.

קָדוֹשׁ, קָדוֹשׁ, קָדוֹשׁ, יְיָ צְבָאוֹת, מְלֹא כָל־הָאָרֶץ כְּבוֹדוֹ.

Holy, holy, holy is *Adonai*, Your glory fills the whole universe.

בָּרוּךְ כְּבוֹד־יְיָ מִמְּקוֹמוֹ.

We praise God's glory from the highest heaven to right here on earth.

יִמְלֹךְ יְיָ לְעוֹלָם, אֱלֹהַיִךְ צִיּוֹן, לְדֹר וָדֹר. הַלְלוּיָהּ!

Adonai, **may You be our God forever,
in each generation, until the end of time.**
Halleluyah!

LEDOR VADOR

May we always be loyal to You, telling the stories of Your greatness, telling the stories of your holiness to our children and their children forever.

בָּרוּךְ אַתָּה, יְיָ, הָאֵל הַקָּדוֹשׁ.

We praise You, *Adonai*, the Holy God.

MAY WE REJOICE – KEDUSHAT HAYOM

The Jewish people shall observe Shabbat always. It is unique, a day we keep as a *brit olam* — an eternal covenant.

Shabbat is a sign — reminding us that God worked six days to create the world.

Shabbat is a sign — reminding us that God rested on the seventh day, making Creation complete.

We, too, must work — using our minds and hands, our ideas and our abilities to create as God creates.

We, too, must rest — stop what we're doing, look at what we've done, and say, as God said, "It is good."

On the seventh day — Shabbat — God stopped and looked around.

God rested; and God blessed the Shabbat day, calling it "the Day of Rest."

וְשָׁמְרוּ בְנֵי־יִשְׂרָאֵל אֶת־הַשַּׁבָּת, לַעֲשׂוֹת אֶת־הַשַּׁבָּת לְדֹרֹתָם בְּרִית עוֹלָם.
בֵּינִי וּבֵין בְּנֵי יִשְׂרָאֵל אוֹת הִיא לְעֹלָם, כִּי שֵׁשֶׁת יָמִים עָשָׂה יְיָ
אֶת־הַשָּׁמַיִם וְאֶת־הָאָרֶץ, וּבַיּוֹם הַשְּׁבִיעִי שָׁבַת וַיִּנָּפַשׁ.

[A SHABBAT SONG]

We close our eyes and pray quietly, saying words without sound.

SILENT PRAYER

**May the words of my mouth echo God's words,
May the thoughts in my heart ever be thoughts of God.** *Amen.*

SERMON

(TORAH SERVICE: PAGE 35)

CLOSING PRAYERS: PAGE 39

TORAH SERVICE

Each day we are supposed to pray. We thank God for our food, our homes, and our families. We pray for love and peace, for learning and wisdom. Before we eat, we say a prayer called *Hamotzi*. After we eat, we say a prayer called *Birkat Hamazon*.

On certain days, we pray in another, especially Jewish way. We read and study Torah. We take the Torah scroll from the Holy Ark, hold it close, and then read its sacred words.

Shabbat is one of those days. Now we take the Torah, march with it, embrace it — some people even kiss it. We love Torah. It is the secret of Jewish life — it is the symbol of who we are and what we believe.

[SONG]

We rise as we open the Holy Ark to show everyone around us that we love and respect the Torah, that we love and respect our religion and our God.

[SONG]

This is our Torah.
    Wherever our people journeyed, they carried it in their arms.
They taught it to their children and tried to live by its teachings.
    We, too, love the Torah; we, too, love our God.
We take the Torah into our arms, promising to study it carefully,
    Promising to listen to its words and teach them to our children.

THE GENERATIONS — MIDOR LEDOR

שְׁמַע יִשְׂרָאֵל: יְיָ אֱלֹהֵינוּ, יְיָ אֶחָד.

Hear, O Israel: The Lord is our God, the Lord is One.

אֶחָד אֱלֹהֵינוּ, גָּדוֹל אֲדוֹנֵינוּ, קָדוֹשׁ שְׁמוֹ.

Our God is One, our Lord is great, God's name is holy.

גַּדְּלוּ לַיְיָ אִתִּי וּנְרוֹמְמָה שְׁמוֹ יַחְדָּו.

O honor the Lord with me; together let us glorify God's name.

[THE TORAH IS READ]

Now that we have read the Torah, we lift it high so that everyone can see what we read.

ALL RISE

וְזֹאת הַתּוֹרָה אֲשֶׁר־שָׂם מֹשֶׁה לִפְנֵי בְּנֵי יִשְׂרָאֵל.

עַל־פִּי יְיָ בְּיַד־מֹשֶׁה.

**This is the Torah that Moses and all the wise teachers
of our people taught us — God's teachings made clear
by our people's teachers.**

Now we dress the Torah carefully. First, we bind it. Then we cover it with a "mantle." We shield it with a breastplate, hang a pointer — the *yad* — on it, and place the sign of royalty on its head. We are ready to return the Torah to the Holy Ark.

[SONG]

עֵץ־חַיִּים הִיא לַמַּחֲזִיקִים בָּהּ, וְתֹמְכֶיהָ מְאֻשָּׁר.
דְּרָכֶיהָ דַרְכֵי־נֹעַם, וְכָל־נְתִיבוֹתֶיהָ שָׁלוֹם.

Eitz chayyim hi — **It is a tree of life
To them that hold fast to it,
And all its supporters are happy.**

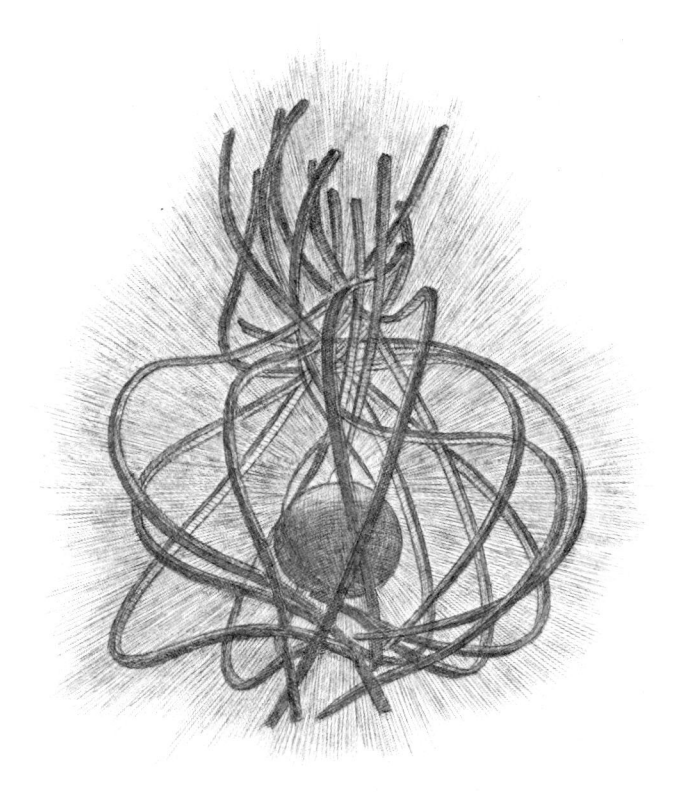

CLOSING PRAYERS

ADORATION

עָלֵינוּ לְשַׁבֵּחַ לַאֲדוֹן הַכֹּל. לָתֵת גְּדֻלָּה לְיוֹצֵר בְּרֵאשִׁית.
שֶׁלֹּא עָשָׂנוּ כְּגוֹיֵי הָאֲרָצוֹת. וְלֹא שָׂמָנוּ כְּמִשְׁפְּחוֹת הָאֲדָמָה:
שֶׁלֹּא שָׂם חֶלְקֵנוּ כָּהֶם. וְגֹרָלֵנוּ כְּכָל־הֲמוֹנָם.

Let us adore the everliving God
    And render praise unto *Adonai*
Who spread out the Heavens and established the earth
    Whose glory is revealed in the Heavens above
And whose greatness is manifest throughout the world
    ***Adonai* is our God, there is none else.**

וַאֲנַחְנוּ כּוֹרְעִים וּמִשְׁתַּחֲוִים וּמוֹדִים
לִפְנֵי מֶלֶךְ מַלְכֵי הַמְּלָכִים. הַקָּדוֹשׁ בָּרוּךְ הוּא.

Va-a-nach-nu Ko-r'im U-mish-ta-cha-vim U-mo-dim
Lif-nei Me-lech Mal-chei Ham-la-chim
Ha-ka-dosh Ba-ruch Hu

We bow the head in reverence
    And worship *Adonai* our God,
The Holy One, *Hakadosh*.

בַּיּוֹם הַהוּא יִהְיֶה יְיָ אֶחָד וּשְׁמוֹ אֶחָד.

Bayom hahu, bayom hahu yihyeh Adonai echad u'shmo echad.

On that day God shall be One,
    And God's name shall be One.

KADDISH

יִתְגַּדַּל וְיִתְקַדַּשׁ שְׁמֵהּ רַבָּא בְּעָלְמָא דִּי־בְרָא כִרְעוּתֵהּ.
וְיַמְלִיךְ מַלְכוּתֵהּ בְּחַיֵּיכוֹן וּבְיוֹמֵיכוֹן וּבְחַיֵּי דְכָל־בֵּית יִשְׂרָאֵל.
בַּעֲגָלָא וּבִזְמַן קָרִיב. וְאִמְרוּ: אָמֵן.
יְהֵא שְׁמֵהּ רַבָּא מְבָרַךְ לְעָלַם וּלְעָלְמֵי עָלְמַיָּא.
יִתְבָּרַךְ וְיִשְׁתַּבַּח. וְיִתְפָּאַר וְיִתְרוֹמַם וְיִתְנַשֵּׂא. וְיִתְהַדָּר וְיִתְעַלֶּה
וְיִתְהַלָּל שְׁמֵהּ דְּקֻדְשָׁא. בְּרִיךְ הוּא. לְעֵלָּא מִן־כָּל־בִּרְכָתָא
וְשִׁירָתָא. תֻּשְׁבְּחָתָא וְנֶחֱמָתָא דַּאֲמִירָן בְּעָלְמָא. וְאִמְרוּ: אָמֵן.
יְהֵא שְׁלָמָא רַבָּא מִן־שְׁמַיָּא וְחַיִּים עָלֵינוּ וְעַל־כָּל־יִשְׂרָאֵל. וְאִמְרוּ: אָמֵן.

Raise high and glorify the name of God
  Throughout the world God chose to create.
May God's kingdom be built
  In your lifetime, during your days,
And in the lifetime of all the House of Israel,
  Soon, and in a time close at hand.
So let us say, Amen.

Let the name of the Holy One, the Blessed,
  Be praised and glorified,
Be exalted, raised up and honored,
  Be magnified and spread.
Though we know God is above all praises,
  Above all songs of praise, and above all blessings,
Above all kind words we speak in our world,
  Even so, we say, Amen.

Let peace pour from the heavens
  With life for us and for all Israel.
So let us say, Amen.

עֹשֶׂה שָׁלוֹם בִּמְרוֹמָיו. הוּא יַעֲשֶׂה שָׁלוֹם
עָלֵינוּ וְעַל־כָּל־יִשְׂרָאֵל. וְאִמְרוּ: אָמֵן.

Creator of peace in the highest places,
  May God create peace for us and for all Israel.
For this, we say, Amen.

ADON OLAM

אֲדוֹן עוֹלָם. אֲשֶׁר מָלַךְ. בְּטֶרֶם כָּל־יְצִיר נִבְרָא.
לְעֵת נַעֲשָׂה בְחֶפְצוֹ כֹּל. אֲזַי מֶלֶךְ שְׁמוֹ נִקְרָא.

וְאַחֲרֵי כִּכְלוֹת הַכֹּל. לְבַדּוֹ יִמְלוֹךְ נוֹרָא.
וְהוּא הָיָה, וְהוּא הֹוֶה, וְהוּא יִהְיֶה בְּתִפְאָרָה.
וְהוּא אֶחָד. וְאֵין שֵׁנִי לְהַמְשִׁיל לוֹ. לְהַחְבִּירָה.
בְּלִי רֵאשִׁית. בְּלִי תַכְלִית. וְלוֹ הָעֹז וְהַמִּשְׂרָה.

וְהוּא אֵלִי. וְחַי גּוֹאֲלִי. וְצוּר חֶבְלִי בְּעֵת צָרָה.
וְהוּא נִסִּי וּמָנוֹס לִי. מְנָת כּוֹסִי בְּיוֹם אֶקְרָא.

בְּיָדוֹ אַפְקִיד רוּחִי בְּעֵת אִישַׁן וְאָעִירָה.
וְעִם־רוּחִי גְּוִיָּתִי: יְיָ לִי. וְלֹא אִירָא.

HAVDALAH

Shabbat is a singular day.
> **Shabbat is a day for thinking.**

Shabbat is a day for singing.
> **Shabbat is a day for hugging.**

Shabbat is a day for being with family and friends.
> **Shabbat is a day for joy.**

[A SHABBAT SONG]

We are so happy as Shabbat begins. We light candles, drink wine, sing songs. We eat special meals. We come to Temple with parents, family, and friends. Shabbat is a day of rest. Shabbat is a day blessed by God.

[A SHABBAT SONG]

We are sad as Shabbat ends. We feel Shabbat slipping away from us. It is like the feeling we have when we say "goodbye" to a friend. We don't want Shabbat to leave.

At the end of Shabbat
> **We drink some wine**

To remind us of sweetness,
> **The sweetness of life,**

The joy of Shabbat.

בָּרוּךְ אַתָּה, יְיָ אֱלֹהֵינוּ, מֶלֶךְ הָעוֹלָם, בּוֹרֵא פְּרִי הַגָּפֶן.

Baruch atah, Adonai — **We praise You,** *Adonai* —
> **Ruler of the universe, Creator of the fruit of the vine.**

At the end of Shabbat
> **We smell some spices**

To remind us
> **Of the special taste,**

The beautiful colors,
> **The lovely flavor,**

The fragrance of Shabbat.

בָּרוּךְ אַתָּה, יְיָ אֱלֹהֵינוּ, מֶלֶךְ הָעוֹלָם, בּוֹרֵא מִינֵי בְשָׂמִים.

Baruch atah, Adonai — **We praise You,** *Adonai* —
Ruler of the universe, Creator of all the spices.

At the end of Shabbat we light a candle,
   A special candle with many wicks,
To remind us of the light of Shabbat —
   The power of light over darkness,
The power of good over evil,
   The light of God.
At the end of Shabbat
   We light a candle with many wicks.

בָּרוּךְ אַתָּה, יְיָ אֱלֹהֵינוּ, מֶלֶךְ הָעוֹלָם, בּוֹרֵא מְאוֹרֵי הָאֵשׁ.

Baruch atah, Adonai — **We praise You,** *Adonai* —
Ruler of the universe, Creator of the flickering fire.

But the candle is so beautiful — Why do we put it out? To remind us that Shabbat must end. Not every day can be Shabbat. We have to work, to go to school, to take care of so many different things. Our lives are very busy. Shabbat must end.

בָּרוּךְ אַתָּה, יְיָ אֱלֹהֵינוּ, מֶלֶךְ הָעוֹלָם, הַמַּבְדִּיל בֵּין קֹדֶשׁ לְחוֹל,

בֵּין אוֹר לְחֹשֶׁךְ, בֵּין יוֹם הַשְּׁבִיעִי לְשֵׁשֶׁת יְמֵי הַמַּעֲשֶׂה.

בָּרוּךְ אַתָּה, יְיָ, הַמַּבְדִּיל בֵּין קֹדֶשׁ לְחוֹל.

Yet the memories of Shabbat stay with us, touching and inspiring us, embracing us during the week.

Darkness will not last.
   Next week Shabbat will come again.
We shall light candles and bless the wine,
   Sing Shabbat songs and eat Shabbat meals.

We hope that a certain special Shabbat will come soon,
> **A Shabbat that will never end — a time of peace and blessing**

For you and me,
> **For all of God's children,**

Yom shekulo Shabbat,
> **A time that is Shabbat forever.**

אֵלִיָּהוּ הַנָּבִיא, אֵלִיָּהוּ הַתִּשְׁבִּי,
אֵלִיָּהוּ, אֵלִיָּהוּ, אֵלִיָּהוּ הַגִּלְעָדִי.
בִּמְהֵרָה בְיָמֵינוּ, יָבֹא אֵלֵינוּ,
עִם מָשִׁיחַ בֶּן דָּוִד, עִם מָשִׁיחַ בֶּן דָּוִד.

Eliyahu Hanavi, Eliyahu Hatishbi
Eliyahu, Eliyahu, Eliyahu Hagiladi
Bimheira, viyameinu, yavo eleinu,
Im Mashiach ben David, im Mashiach ben David.

שָׁבוּעַ טוֹב . . .

Shavua Tov
A good week, a week of peace,
May gladness reign and joy increase.

BJE/RMC
006809